MATHS QUEST

The CAVERN of CLUES

DAVID GLOVER

QED Publishing

Illustrator: Tim Hutchinson
Editor: Lauren Taylor
Designer: Maria Bowers

Language consultant: Penny Glover

First published in the UK in 2011 by
QED Publishing
A Quarto Group company
226 City Road
London EC1V 2TT

www.qed-publishing.co.uk

A catalogue record for this book is available from the British Library.

ISBN 978 1 84835 635 1

Printed in China

How to begin your quest

Are you ready for an amazing adventure – with twists and turns, exciting action and puzzles to solve? Then this is the book for you!

The Cavern of Clues is no ordinary book – you don't read the pages in order, 1, 2, 3... Instead you must jump to and fro, forwards and back, as the plot unfolds. Sometimes you may lose your way, but the story will soon guide you back to where you need to be.

The story begins on page 4. Very soon you will have problems to solve and choices to make. The choices will look something like this:

If you think the correct answer is A, go to page 10

If you think the correct answer is B, go to page 18

Your task is to solve each problem and make the right choice. So, if you think the correct answer is A, you turn to page 10 and look for the symbol. That's where you will find the next part of the story.

But what happens if you make the wrong choice? Don't worry! The text will explain where you went wrong and send you back to try again.

The problems in this quest are all about calculations. To solve them you must use your addition, subtraction, multiplication and division skills. To help you, there is a glossary of calculation words at the back of the book, starting on page 44. You will find all the calculation methods and ideas you need there.

As you follow the adventure you will collect a ring and other objects to put in the bag you are carrying. Make a note of the objects as you find them. You will need them all to complete the quest successfully.

So do you think you are ready? Turn the page and let your adventure begin!

Welcome to the Cavern of Clues

You are on a thrilling jungle tour with your friends. You're all enjoying the hot sun and beautiful wildlife when you hear the sound of fluttering wings from above. A scroll of parchment suddenly drops from the sky into your hands. It's a pirate treasure map! You can't resist following it!

But have you done the right thing? The map takes you to the Cavern of Clues. It's dark and spooky inside. You look down at the treasure map. Its riddles could lead you to pirate gold. If you solve the clues the treasure will be yours, but if you fail, you might be trapped in the Cavern forever!

First you must find the four secret signs of the four pirate brothers – Grey Beard, Red Beard, Blue Beard and Black Beard. Only then will the path to the gold be clear.

If you are ready for the challenge, go to page 14 

If you are still not sure, go to page 29 

To find Red Beard's secret sign you must scare the pirates from the Cavern. But first you must find them!

Some of the handprints are pointing left, others are pointing right. You see an instruction painted on the rocks. The hands have fractions written on them!

Three hands show,
Which way to go,
Three equal fractions,
In a row.

If you turn left, go to page 40 

If you turn right, go to page 9 

0.5

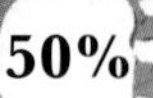

0.4

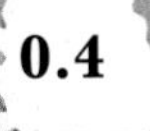

1/4

40%

You nod to yourself. Red Beard has got it right.

Thirteen each is fair, but Red Beard keeps the remaining 5 for himself – the other pirates don't like that!

Go to page 19 

You climb aboard a truck on the left track and push off. The truck gathers speed! Ahead you see a huge empty space. The tunnel has collapsed into the mouth of an underground volcano! Molten rock bubbles and spits hundreds of metres below!

Feeling desperate, you look around. You find a rusty handle on the side of the truck. It's the brake! You pull it hard. The truck screeches to a stop on the edge of the crater. You jump down from the truck and climb slowly back up the track to safety.

You chose the wrong direction! $11 \times 9 = 99$ and $12 \times 8 = 96$. So, the correct statement is: '$11 \times 9 > 12 \times 8$'. The symbol $>$ means 'greater than'.

Go to page 29 

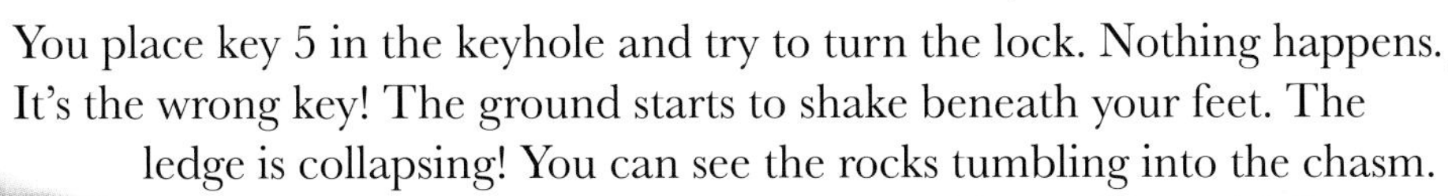

You place key 5 in the keyhole and try to turn the lock. Nothing happens. It's the wrong key! The ground starts to shake beneath your feet. The ledge is collapsing! You can see the rocks tumbling into the chasm. Soon the spot where you stand will crumble and fall!

The missing number will make the second number greater than 50, so it must make the first number less than 50 to give a total of 100. Quickly – try again!

Go to page 16 

It's the right torch! As you lift it down from the wall, it glows more brightly. You set off boldly along the tunnel.

Wait – is that the sound of wings? Is something following you?

Go to page 23 

It's the right gap. You see daylight ahead! A good estimate for 39×61 is $40 \times 60 = 2400$.

Go to page 18 

You see a stack of cannon balls between two cannons. The balls are numbered.

A slip of paper has been pushed between the balls. You pull it out and read the message...

Find two balls that total 500.
Load the cannons – but be sure you're right!
If you are wrong, you'll start a fight!

If you choose balls 225 and 275, go to page 17 

If you choose balls 175 and 225, go to page 16 

3, 6, 12,

It's the correct number! You add it to the numbers in your notebook so you don't forget.

As you look ahead, a glimmer of light catches your eye. It's the reflection of your candle from an underground river!

The river looks dark, deep and cold. It's flowing fast through the cave. The clue said that you will not find the sign if you stay on solid ground, so you guess you must take to the water. But how? It's too cold and dangerous to swim.

Then you see it – a wooden rowing boat! It looks old and rotten, but it's still afloat. The boat is fastened by a long chain. A wooden sign gives an instruction...

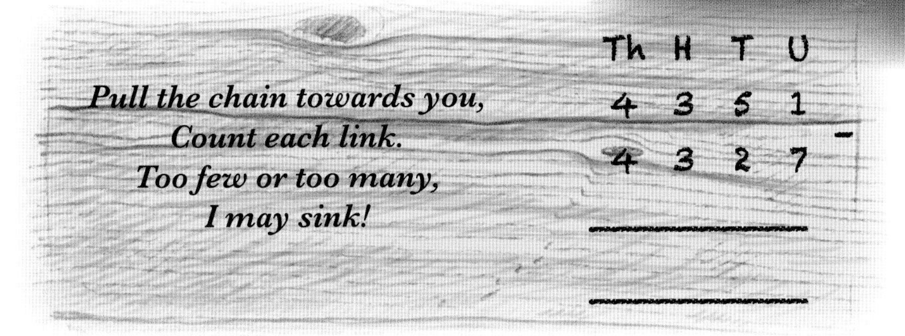

You guess the answer to the subtraction problem is the number you need. You pull the chain, counting the links one at a time: 1, 2, 3…

If you count 34 links, go to page 23 

If you count 24 links, go to page 38 

Now that you have Red Beard's sign you race back to the entrance to explore another part of the Cavern. There is no sign of the pirates. The bear has chased them into the jungle.

Go to page 14 

A path leads up the mountainside through the jungle. You see a sign ahead. You must return to the entrance to explore another part of the Cavern.

Go to page 14

You take the candle and carry on down the passageway. Suddenly a loud squawk stops you in your tracks. One more step and you would have plunged into a chasm! You peer down by the light of the candle, but you cannot see the bottom.

You look at the treasure map. The chasms are marked on it. A diagram shows you how to get across...

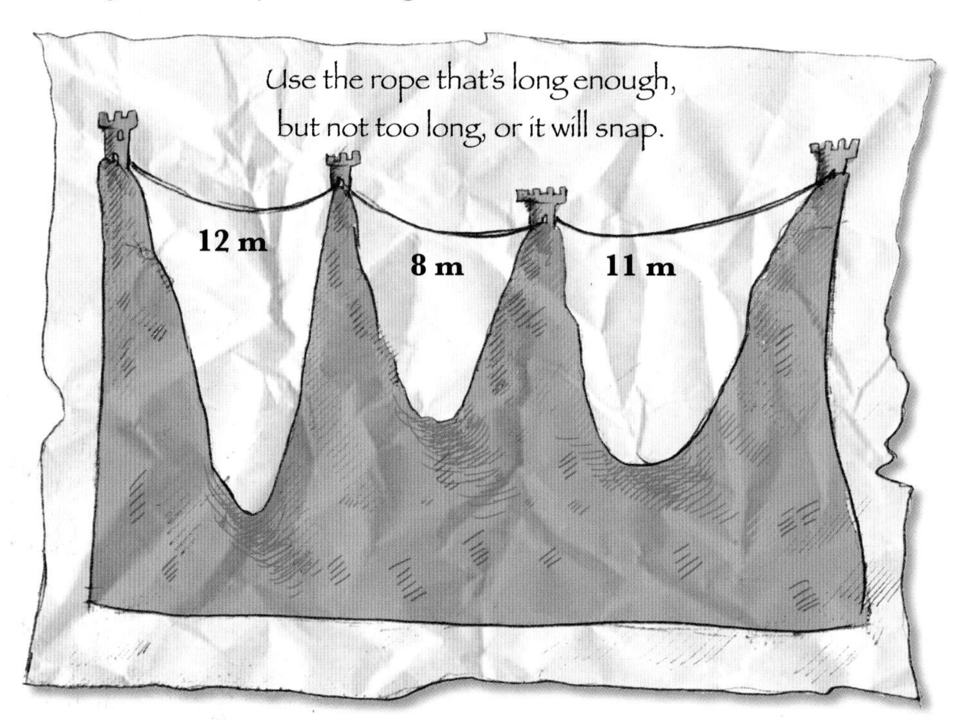

You find three ropes at the edge. Which rope equals the sum of all three chasms and will reach across to the other side?

If you choose the 29 m rope, go to page 37 

If you choose the 31 m rope, go to page 17 

If you choose the 33 m rope, go to page 33 

You tug at the knots, but they just seem to get tighter. Perhaps you are wrong and you will be trapped forever!

Quick – check that you have the signs in the correct order!

Go to page 34 

On the other side of the web, the tunnel splits in two. Which way have the pirates gone? Their footprints have been brushed away.

Then you see numbers painted on the tunnel floor. Perhaps they are something to do with the mine plan?

Which passage should you take? A hot draught carries a swirl of dust and litter around your feet. You see a scrap from the mine engineer's notebook. It's a long multiplication problem, only partly finished. You need to complete the calculation to tell which number tunnel to take.

If you head down passage 1264, go to page 31

If you head down passage 1284, go to page 42

You have chosen the right direction! Ahead the tunnel descends steeply. There are steps cut in the rock. You start to climb down them.

Go to page 36 

You follow the map into the Tunnel of Fear. You pause nervously at the entrance. A cold wind whistles along the passage. The hairs on the back of your neck stand up… Then you hear the gentle flap of wings behind you. For some reason you don't feel afraid. You step forwards with more confidence.

Go to page 28

You creep out of the cage and along the passageway. There is a stack of barrels. It's gunpowder! Blue Beard and his crew are going to blast the tunnel! They want to find the last remaining diamonds.

You hide behind the barrels. Then you see a screwed-up piece of paper. It's the instructions for using the gunpowder – the pirates have lost them! The pirates are building a huge pile of barrels for the blast. Are they using too many?

Each barrel is labelled 3.5 kg. You count 14 barrels in the pile. You calculate the charge the pirates have set.

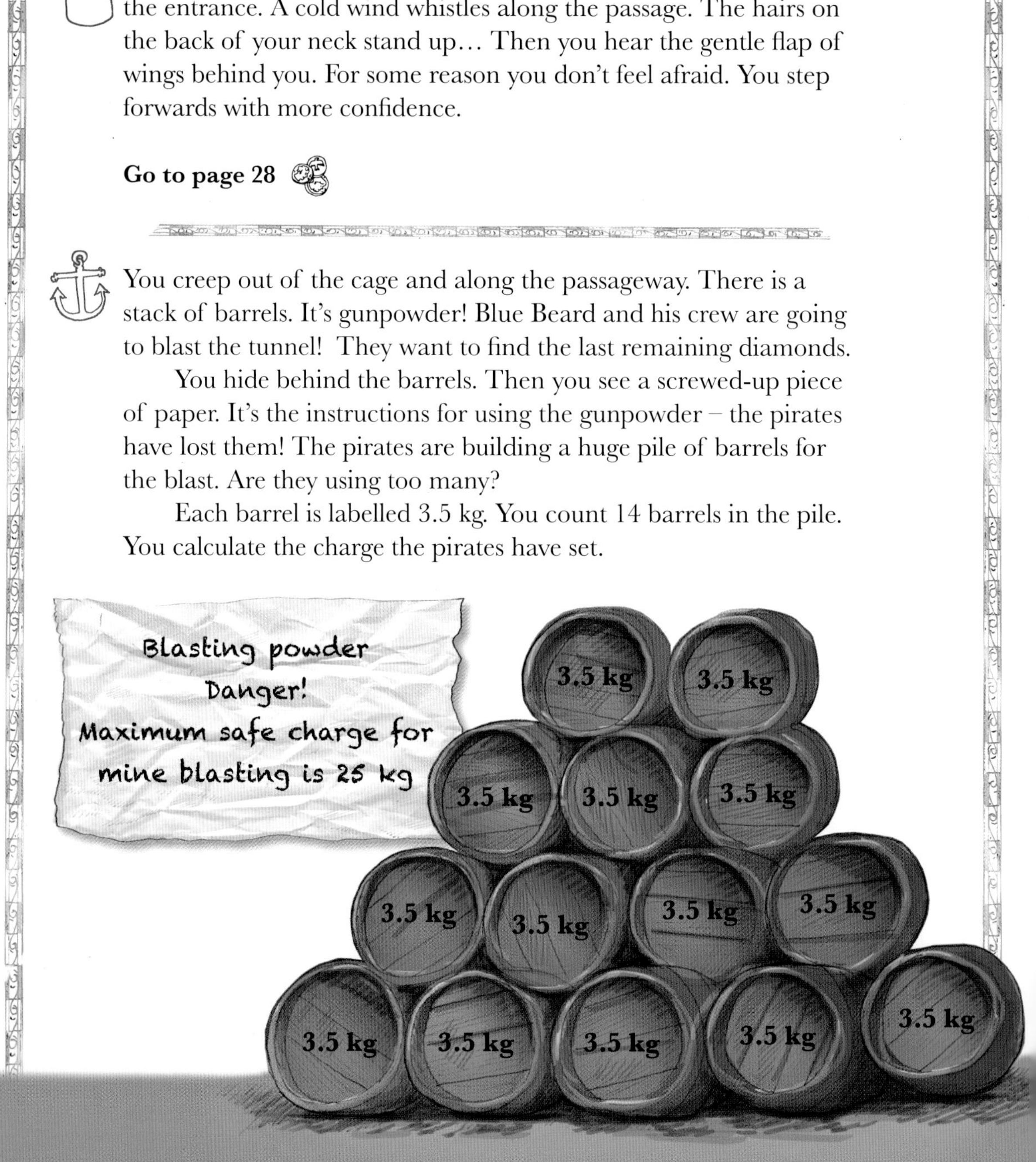

If you think the explosion will be unsafe, go to page 38 

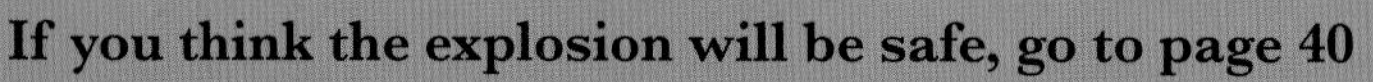

If you think the explosion will be safe, go to page 40 

They are the right stones! ($6 \times 6 = 36$, $9 \times 4 = 36$, $3 \times 12 = 36$.) You step from stone to stone until you are safely across.

Go to page 27

You creep around the cave behind the row of barrels. The barrels are numbered on the back, but the label showing what each barrel contains is at the front – on the same side as the pirates. You can't remember which contains the honey!

Then you see a note chalked on the wall...

Honey in barrel number = 253 ÷ 11

If you think the honey is in barrel 21, go to page 30 

If you think the honey is in barrel 23, go to page 28

It's the right number! As you say it, the captain's hand rises. The ring slips from his finger and rolls across the table. You grab it and race back the way you have come – down the ship's side, across the lake, through the cave, along the ledge, across the rope and back to the entrance! That was fast work! Now you need to take another tunnel in the Cavern.

Go to page 14

This is it, the entrance to the Tunnel of No Return. The pirates' gold is waiting inside, but do you have the courage and skill to claim it?

Then, as if from nowhere, a beautiful parrot lands on your shoulder. It's a scarlet macaw called Pollygone – she's been helping you all along!

"Have no fear! Have no fear! Pollygone is here!" the parrot cries. Pollygone's cheeky voice gives you courage. You step forwards into the tunnel.

Go to page 38 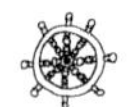

The river passes through spectacular caves. Ahead you see that the river flows into a huge pool – it's an underground lake, and floating at the centre is an ancient pirate ship!

At that moment, something bumps into your boat. You look over the side and see a floating barrel. You pull it from the water. A pirate has scratched some words on the barrel...

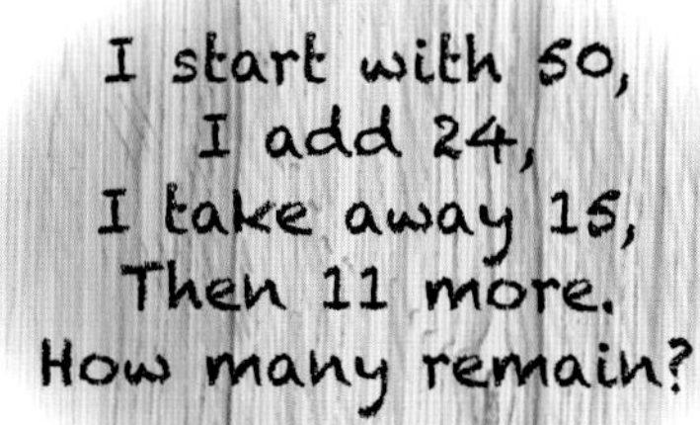

You guess that the answer is another number you will need in your quest.

If you think the number is 48, go to page 21

If you think the number is 52, go to page 40

You chose the right number! You count out four matches. You strike one and light the lamp.

Go to page 36

You have taken the correct number (80 ÷ 5 = 16). You just manage to carry all the planks and lay them one at a time across the pools. Soon you have reached the other side.

Go to page 39 

On the far side of the chasm you find yourself on a narrow ledge. But which way should you go – left or right? You are still holding the candle. You dare not take your other hand from the wall to look at the map – you could easily tumble back into the dark depths below!

Then you see a message chalked on the rock...

Follow the greater sum!

If this sum is greater, turn left

Th	H	T	U	
4	4	1	2	+
3	5	3	6	

____

____

≠

If this sum is greater, turn right

Th	H	T	U	
5	3	5	8	+
2	5	3	2	

____

____

If you turn left, go to page 41 

If you turn right, go to page 39 

The treasure map shows that four tunnels lead from the Cavern entrance. An X marks the site of the treasure. Which tunnel should you take?

The blast has left a huge pile of rocks across the tunnel. Then you spot two gaps at the top. Which should you take? As you climb you glimpse the sparkle of diamonds in the rocks. Then you see a message scratched in the dust, as if by a feather.

If you take gap 2400, go to page 6

If you take gap 2500, go to page 41

Little does Black Beard know, but you have collected all three signs in your adventures.

Boldly you reply, "Yes, I'll share your treasure, Black Beard. But first you must give me that belt with the golden buckle."

Black Beard starts to smile – his trick is working. He thinks you are tempted by the sight of gold! He takes off his belt and passes it to you across the ropes. As you grab the end, he tugs you inside the rings and leaps out.

Black Beard roars with laughter. "You can have the treasure, m'hearty – much good may it do you if you're trapped here forever!"

With a wave of his hat he is gone – back to the freedom of the high seas. But now you have the fourth sign!

Go to page 34

You are inside a chamber in the rocks. It feels surprisingly warm. Then you hear the sound of strong breathing. It's coming from a large mound in the corner. You step closer and look. It's a huge Grizzly Bear fast asleep! You can see his long sharp claws. He has yellow teeth like daggers!

The bear is stirring! How can you keep him asleep? Then you see a message written on the wall.

Count gently to keep Great Bear asleep.
If he wakes, it's you he'll eat!
Count to the missing number here:
$500 \div ? = 5$
Then escape without fear.

If you count to 50, go to page 26

If you count to 100, go to page 29

You roll the balls into the cannons. They are the wrong ones! With a huge roar, both cannons fire – it's a signal! The pirate skeletons come to life. They wave their pistols and cutlasses, gather together and start to come for you. Run for your life!

Then you spot something fly up to the top of the mast. Ropes are pulled. The sail crashes down, trapping the pirate band underneath. Someone is helping you!

The sum of 175 and 225 is 400, not 500.

Go to page 6

On a hook next to the gate you find a set of rusty keys. There is a label attached to the key ring with an instruction…

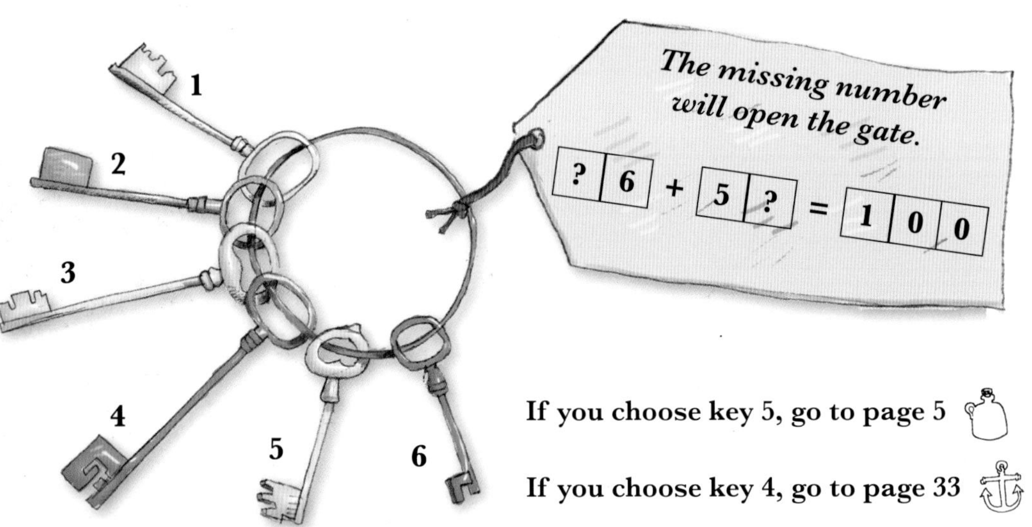

If you choose key 5, go to page 5

If you choose key 4, go to page 33

You avoid plank Y. You are about to step on plank X when a loud squawk warns you not to. X is the weak plank, not Y. The answer to 6 × 150 is 900. Plank 900 is towards the end of the number line.

Go to page 18

You throw the rope across the chasm. It just reaches the other side. The hook bites into a crack in the rock. You secure the rope, and drag yourself along, one hand over the other. You are across! It was the right rope!

Go to page 13 

You roll the balls into the cannons. They are the right ones! The extra weight makes the cannons roll down the sloping deck. They gather speed, and crash through a door next to the ship's wheel. It's the captain's cabin!

Go to page 32 

You carry on to the end of the passage. It opens into the pirates' secret cave. It's filled with barrels of food, sacks of spices, rolls of silk and chests full of stolen goods. The pirates are gathered in a circle around their captain – Red Beard!

Red Beard is sharing out piles of coins. But is he doing it fairly? You hear Red Beard say there are 200 doubloons to go round. There are 15 pirates in the band including him. He gives everyone 13 each. There are 5 left over. Some of the pirates are saying that Red Beard has made a mistake.

If you think the division is correct, go to page 5

If you think the division is wrong, go to page 39

As you climb through the gap you hear the pirates climbing behind you. But wait – they are stopping! They have spotted the diamonds! Only Blue Beard continues the chase.

Ahead you see that the tunnel opens out into the side of a gorge in the jungle. There is a rickety rope bridge crossing the chasm. Will it take your weight? Then you see a sign on the bridge...

Most of my planks are strong,
But step on 6 x 150 and
you'll be gone!

You see that the planks across the bridge are numbered in tens. They make a number line with 10 at one end and 1000 at the other. Where is plank 6 × 150?

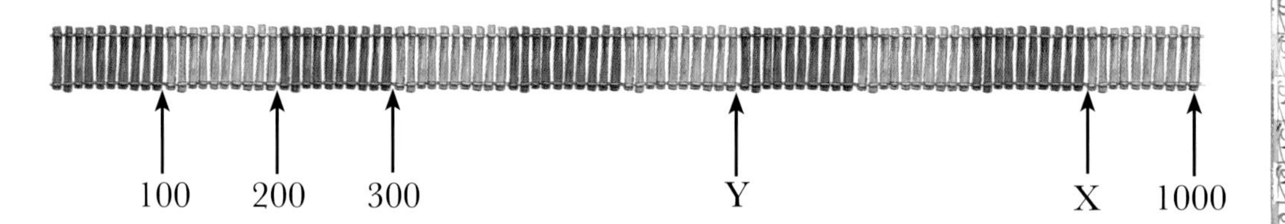

If you think 6 × 150 is at X, go to page 41 

If you think 6 × 150 is at Y, go to page 16 

You start to say the number 96... The captain's eyes glow red. His bony hand reaches for a dagger. Then a loud squawk stops you finishing the word. It was the wrong number!

The rule for the series is 'double the last number to find the next number'. The number 96 is the next number in the series, not the next but one. What is double 96?

Go to page 32 

A short distance ahead, the tunnel opens out. You step forwards and hold up the candle. In the flickering light you see that you have entered a huge cave. The roof soars overhead like a dome. There's something moving up there! You hear squeaks and the sound of wings. Then you see them! There are hundreds of huge bats, some hanging like hairy fruits, others flapping and swooping around in all directions.

On the ground ahead lies a stone slab. There is a skull and crossbones carved at the top, and a chilling message underneath...

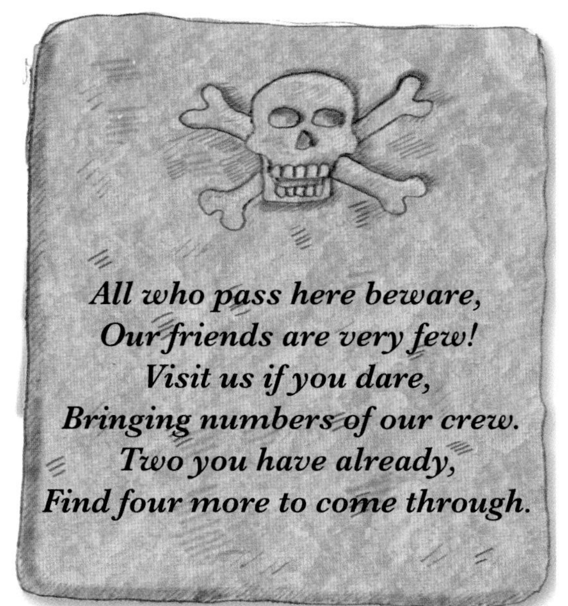

Go to page 30 

The pirates' argument gets louder. This is your chance! If you can surprise them and scare them from the cave, then you can claim the pirate's sign!

But how can you scare them? You look around the things in the cave. Then you see it – a barrel labelled 'honey'! That's it! A barrel of honey and a giant bear are just what you need!

Go to page 11

The truck comes to a rest by a cage at the top of a deep shaft. That's where the voices are coming from – they are working down below.

The cage is a lift. It travels up and down the mine shaft carrying miners and their tools. There is a sign on the cage door with instructions and a multiplication chart...

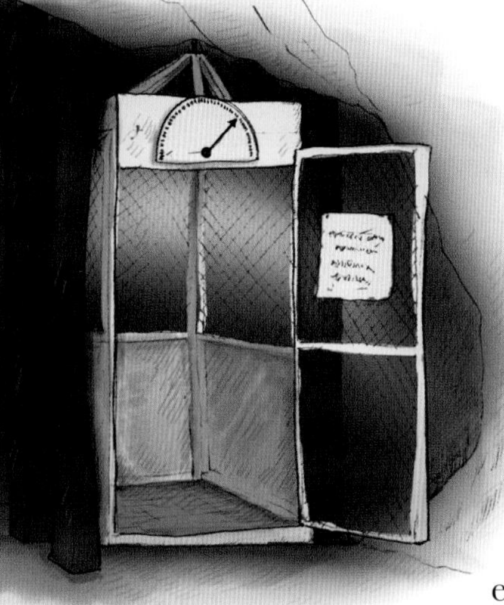

To find the last diamonds in this mine,
Take me down to level **V**
Turn my handle, but beware,
Do not stop at level **T**!

You must work out what 'V' and 'T' equal using the multiplication chart. Then you can take the lift to the right level!

X	1	2	3	4	5	6	7	8	9	10
7	7	14	21	V	35	42	49	56	63	70
8	8	16	24	32	40	48	56	64	72	80
9	9	18	T	36	45	54	63	72	81	90

If you are going to stop at level 28, go to page 30

If you are going to stop at level 27, go to page 21

They are the correct numbers! Each row adds up to 20.

You take your notepad from your bag and write the numbers down. The message said you will need them 'when you find the pirate crew'.

Go to page 8

The tunnel ahead is pitch-black. But at the entrance you find an oil lamp and a box of matches. You pick up the matchbox to light the lamp. Then you see an instruction on the box.

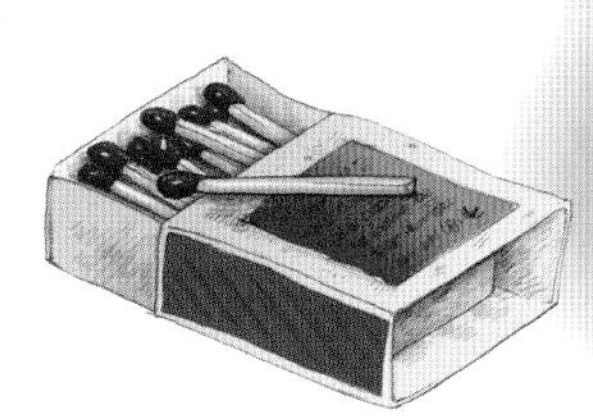

There are 24 matches in this box.
You are one of six people who will share them.
Take your share, no more no less, then the lamp will light.

If you take 6 matches from the box, go to page 35 

If you take 4 matches from the box, go to page 13 

You climb into the cage and turn the handle. The cage descends. A needle moves along a scale to show your level. At level 27 you stop turning and open the door.

Huge hairy arms reach inside the cage! Knobbly hands with ragged black nails grab at you. You jump to the back of the cage. Something screeches and flies at the monster. For a moment the arms pull back and you manage to close the door.

You made the wrong choice! 3 × 9 is 27!

Go to page 20 

It's the right number! You add the number 48 to the list in your note book. Can you see a pattern?

You pick up the oars and row on towards the pirate ship.

Go to page 35

You follow the running crew. There is a huge flash, followed by a loud roar. You dive for cover behind a boulder. A cloud of dust billows down the tunnel. All the pirates start to cough and rub their eyes.

You peep around the boulder. Blue Beard is right next to you! You see a gold medallion hanging from his neck. It's his pirate sign! Can you reach it while Blue Beard is blinded by the dust?

Like a flash you spring up, snatch the medallion from his neck and race back down the tunnel.

Blue Beard roars in surprise – then he and his pirates come after you!

Go to page 14 

Quickly you untie all four ropes and throw them to one side. The pirate curse is broken! The treasure is yours to take!

Pollygone hops up and down, calling, "Pieces of eight! Pieces of eight!"

But wait – you hear footsteps behind you. Someone isn't very happy that you solved the puzzle...

Go to page 25 

You look more closely at the map to get your bearings. You notice something written near the tunnel entrance…

If you have three pirate signs, go to page 12

If you do not have three pirate signs, go to page 14

You've pulled the boat too far! It scrapes against a rock. It will be holed! Then a big swirl of water flows past. The chain is pulled from your hands and the boat is washed back to where it started.

Try the subtraction again – don't forget to decrease the 5 to 4, when you increase the 1 to 11.

Th	H	T	U
4	3	$^{4}5$	$^{1}1$
4	3	2	7

Go to page 7 

Ahead you see a wide crack across the tunnel floor. You step cautiously up to the edge. A river of molten lava is blocking your way. The lava is red hot, you cannot step across! Then you see stones sticking out, like stepping stones. But are they safe?

You look for a clue. It's on the first stone, and the other stones all have multiplications scratched on them, too!

If you step on stones 3 × 12 and 9 × 4, go to page 11

If you step on stones 9 × 6 and 8 × 4, go to page 42

You turn around and Black Beard is striding back towards you with a cutlass in his hand! “If I couldn’t solve that puzzle, then no one can!” he cries.

Suddenly Pollygone flies to your rescue. She swoops down and picks up a rope. She flies around Black Beard, tying him up! You are safe!

You pick up a handful of gold coins. But what good are they to you? It’s no fun sitting with a pile of stolen gold forever – Black Beard discovered that! Freedom is more important than all the treasure in the world. You pop one gold coin in your pocket for luck, and then you turn your back on the treasure. With your new friend, Pollygone, you are sure that many more adventures are just around the corner.

THE END

The Tunnel of Doom is lit by blazing torches. There is a strong smell – a mixture of fireworks and rotten eggs. A blast of hot air hits your face. In the distance you hear strange sounds. There are low rumbles, gloops, gurgles and sudden hisses.

Ahead someone has drawn an arrow on the floor with a message…

Blue Beard – one of the pirate brothers! You need his sign to complete your quest. Then you notice the torches that line the wall are numbered. You must take one of the torches to find your way!

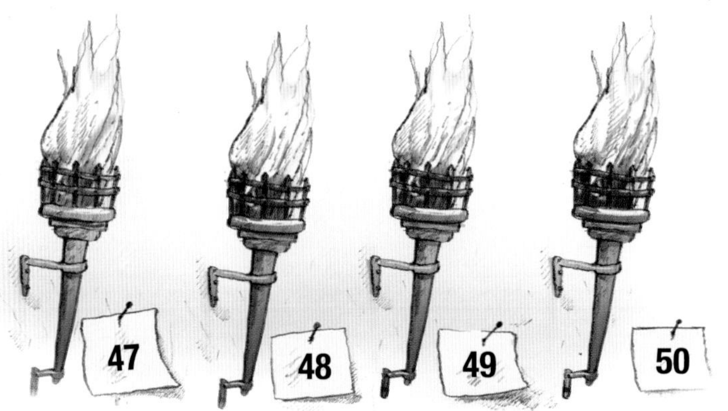

If you take torch 47, go to page 43

If you take torch 49, go to page 6

You have not counted far enough! The bear starts to wake: he's going to see you! If you divide 500 by 50 the answer is 10. You must divide 500 by 100 to get 5. Someone carries on counting for you. The bear's eyes close again. Who was that?

Go to page 15

The candle goes out. You are stranded in the dark! You chose the wrong numbers! One row is complete, $9 + 9 + 2 = 20$. So the numbers in the other rows must add to 20 as well.

You hear wings flapping. A match lights the candle. Who did that?

Go to page 28 

You look more closely at the pirate knots.

"You will never untie them without my brothers' signs!" cries Black Beard. "I know, I've tried!"

Go to page 15 

Now the tunnel begins to descend steeply. The air gets hotter and the sounds grow louder. You see footprints in the dirt ahead. What's that shining? It's a pirate cutlass, lying on the ground. This is where Blue Beard and his band have come searching for the diamonds!

Just ahead something is blocking the tunnel. It's a huge cobweb! There is no way past. Then you see a message scrawled in the dust...

Find the missing numbers
at high speed.
The spider is coming for a feed!

$35 \times 10 = \boxed{?}$

$35 \times \boxed{?} = 35{,}000$

If you think the missing numbers are 350 and 1000, go to page 41

If you think the missing numbers are 3500 and 100, go to page 32

The passageway ahead is as black as night. The only sound is your heart thumping in your chest. Then, somewhere in the depths, a point of light appears. You walk towards it.

You find a candle flickering in a crevice in the wall. There's a message written in the soot from the flame...

The sign you seek cannot be found,
By one who stays on solid ground.
You will need these numbers two,
When you find the pirate crew.

Find the two numbers
that make each diagonal
row of three add up
to the same sum.

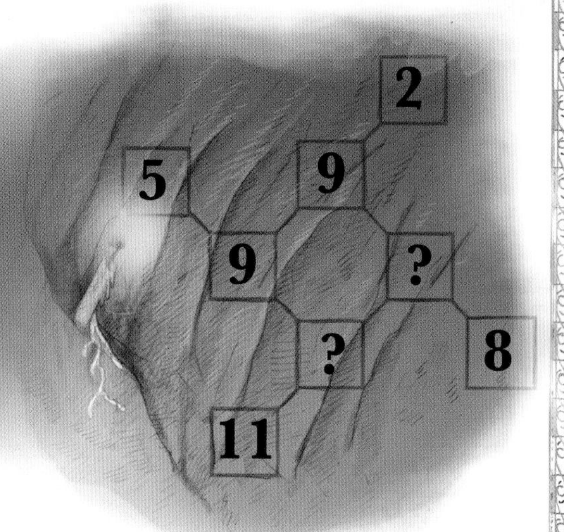

If you think the numbers are 3 and 6, go to page 20 

If you think the numbers are 4 and 7, go to page 27 

It's the right barrel! You pull the cork from the top and the honey starts to drip out. As you roll the barrel it leaves a trail of honey on the ground. You roll it along the passageway and into the bear's den. With a final heave, you push the barrel towards the bear.

The bear wakes and smells the honey! It licks its lips and starts to follow the trail, lapping with its huge tongue as it goes.

Go to page 33

Don't be afraid. It's a challenging adventure, but help is nearby. When you are stuck or in danger, a mysterious friend will guide you and keep you safe. Just follow the instructions, one at a time, and see how far you get. You may be surprised by how much you know! Good luck.

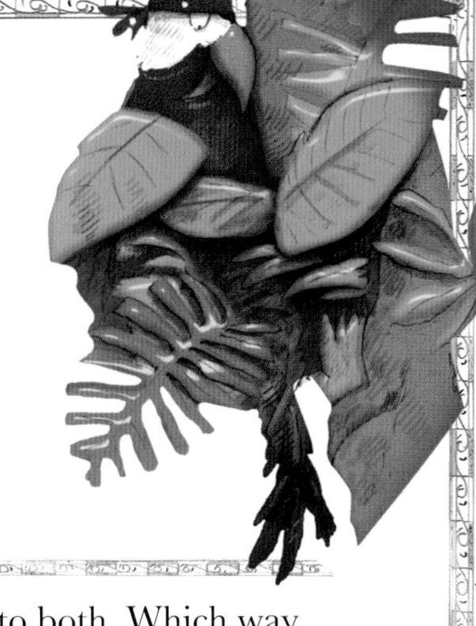

Go to page 14

There are two exits from the cave. The rails run into both. Which way should you go? Then you see a message scratched on the back of an old mine truck...

Is 11 × 9 greater or less than 12 × 8?
Choose the sign that makes this statement correct:

11 × 9 ***?*** ***12 × 8***

greater than >: go right
less than < : go left

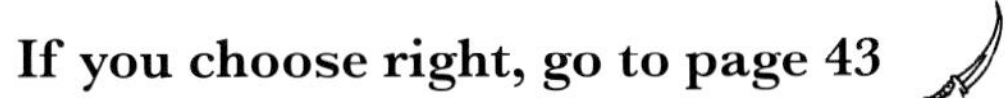

If you choose right, go to page 43 

If you choose left, go to page 5 

As you count to 100 the bear starts to snore loudly. You creep silently from his den, taking care not to wake him.

Go to page 17

You chose the wrong barrel! This barrel is full of nails. As you roll it away, the nails rattle. The pirates hear the sound and look around. Then there is a loud squawk.

"Just the parrot making noises," says Red Beard. But you can see that Red Beard's parrot is fast asleep! The pirates go back to their argument.

Try setting the calculation out like the example below, and see what answer you get.

11   253

Go to page 11

Next to the slab there is a subtraction problem chalked on the rock. Perhaps this will give you one more of the numbers you need!

You see a piece of chalk, so you pick it up and write a number to complete the problem.

If you write 18, go to page 42 

If you write 12, go to page 7 

You climb into the cage and turn the handle. The cage descends. A needle moves on a scale to show your level. At level 28 you stop turning and open the door. You made the right choice! The voices are louder now. You can see movement at the end of the passageway.

Go to page 10

You look at the map and find the entrance to the Tunnel of Despair. On the map there is a description...

The entrance is straight ahead. It's narrow and frightening. You wonder if you are brave enough to go in. Then a friendly voice calls your name. You look around, but all you see is a colourful feather fluttering from the tunnel – as if a bird has just flown inside. Feeling more confident you follow the sound.

Go to page 21

At first the tunnel descends, but then it starts to rise again. That seems odd. Suddenly you hear a rumbling sound ahead. You look up and see a huge boulder rolling straight at you! A loud squawk attracts your attention. There is a narrow crack in the wall, just big enough to squeeze inside. Just in time! The boulder scrapes the wall as it rolls past.

It was the wrong number. Don't forget to carry over when you do long multiplication.

Th	H	T	U	
	2	1	4	
			6	×
1	2	8	4	
1		2		

Go to page 9

You use your finger to write the numbers 3500 and 100 in the spaces. A huge spider crawls onto the web and heads towards you. You snatch up the cutlass – the spider backs away.

They are the wrong numbers! When you multiply by 10 you add one zero to a number; adding three zeros means you have multiplied by 1000. Quickly, try the problems again!

Go to page 27 

The pirate captain is sitting at his table. It's Grey Beard, one of the pirate brothers, but he is a skeleton too! His bony hand rests on the ship's logbook. On his finger you see a huge gold ring. The ring is his sign! You reach for the ring, but his hand will not move from the book. Then you see an instruction written on the page...

Before I give my ring to you,
Say the number of my crew.
The number you need is next but one,
In the series you've begun.

A series you've begun – it must be the numbers you have collected on your journey through the Tunnel of Fear.

3, 6, 12, 24, 48

If you think the number of the crew is 96, go to page 18

If you think the number of the crew is 192, go to page 11

You throw the rope across the chasm. It reaches the other side easily (but was it too easily?) The hook bites into a crack in the rock. You tie the rope securely, and drag yourself along, one hand over the other. Suddenly the rope in front of you starts to fray and part. You are going to fall! You hang onto the rope as it snaps, and swing down into empty space. Luckily your knot holds as you climb back up to the edge of the chasm.

That was close! It was the wrong rope!

Go to page 8 

The bear reaches the pirates' cave. It sees all the food and gives a mighty roar.

The pirates jump like frightened rabbits – they are not so brave and fearsome after all! They see the huge bear heading towards them, and panic. They run for their lives down the tunnel. You stay hidden in the shadows. As he flees past you, Red Beard's hat flies from his head into your hands.

Pinned to the hat you find a gold badge. It carries a sign. It's Red Beard's sign of the pirate brothers!

Go to page 7

You place key 4 in the keyhole. It's the right one! The lock turns easily. You push the gate open and you are through. Something flutters through the open gate after you – what was that?

Go to page 19

Attached to each of the pirates' knots is a label bearing a calculation. But the calculation signs are missing! Now you understand. You must use the pirate signs to complete the calculations.

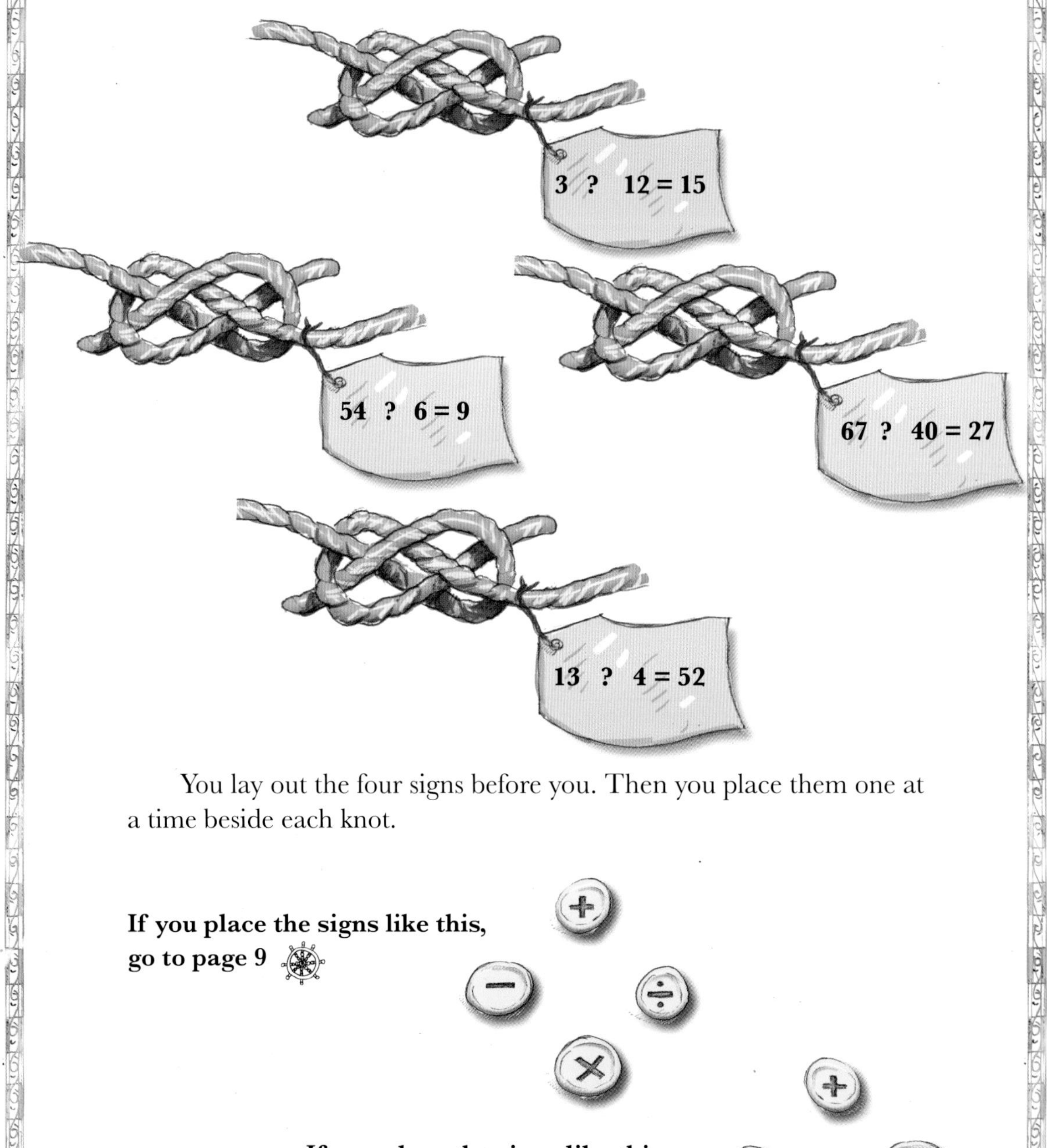

You lay out the four signs before you. Then you place them one at a time beside each knot.

If you place the signs like this, go to page 9

If you place the signs like this, go to page 37

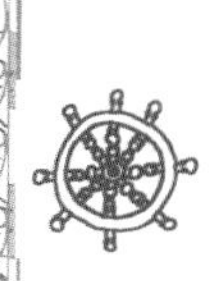

You count out six matches. You take one match and strike it, but the flame dies before you can light the lamp. You are left in the dark.

You try another match. It lights. You glimpse something long slithering towards you through the tunnel, but the flame goes out. The slithering sound continues! The third match goes out too – you must have taken the wrong number!

To share 24 between 6 you must do a division calculation ($24 \div 6 = 4$).

Quickly you put two matches back. Your final match lights the lamp. As the tunnel lights up, something slithers away into the distance.

Go to page 36 

As you approach the pirate ship, you think you can hear singing and laughter. The pirates are on board. But then everything goes quiet.

You row up to the side of the ship, where a rope ladder is hanging down. Quietly, you climb it. You reach the deck and look around. There are no pirates – only skeletons dressed in ragged pirate clothes. This pirate crew is long dead!

You must have imagined the noise. Now you must find the signs of the pirate brothers.

Go to page 6

You hold up the lamp. You see that the tunnel divides. The walls are covered with prehistoric paintings. People lived here once! There are paintings of animals and hunters like stick men with spears. There are human handprints. Among the paintings you see a message...

Once this cave was our home,
But now we are not alone.
Pirates come in here at night,
To stash their booty out of sight.

Scare the pirates from their den,
And we can rest in peace again.
The pirate sign will be yours,
When Red Beard is frightened
by sharp claws.

Go to page 4

At the bottom of the steps you find yourself in a cave. There is no floor, just a series of cold dark pools. There is no way across. Then you see a pile of planks. You must use the planks to cross the pools. But how many will you need?

Someone has chalked information on one of the planks...

Width of cave: 80 metres
Length of planks: 5 metres each

If you take too many planks you will not be able to carry the weight. If you take too few planks you will get stuck.

If you need 16 planks, go to page 13 

If you need 18 planks, go to page 37 

You throw the rope across the chasm. It does not reach the other side – the rope is too short! Calculate again and try another one!

Go to page 8

You tug at the knots. They start to unravel at your touch! You placed the signs correctly.

Go to page 22

You pick up the planks, and stagger towards the pools. They are so heavy that you topple and fall into the water. As you sink, flashes of silver catch your eye. A shoal of piranhas is circling around you!

Luckily one of the planks falls into the water with you. You grab it and float back to the surface. Quickly you drag yourself from the water before the piranhas attack.

You collected too many planks. To find out how many you need, you must divide the length of the cave by the length of each plank: 80 ÷ 5 = ? You could set out this calculation as a long division like this:

$$\begin{array}{r} 16 \\ 5 \overline{)80} \\ -\underline{5} \\ 30 \end{array}$$

Go to page 36

You pull up 24 links of the chain. The boat is just in reach and you jump aboard. Before you untie the rope that holds the chain, you make a note of the number in your book.

You grab the oars and row out into the current.

3, 6, 12, 24

Go to page 12

You are right – the pirates are using too much gunpowder! (3.5 × 14 = 49.) 49 kg is nearly twice the safe amount. The whole tunnel will collapse!

The pirates finish piling the barrels. Blue Beard is about to light the fuse. Quick – you must do something!

Then there is a rustle of feathers. The gunpowder instructions are snatched from your hand. Just as Blue Beard stoops to light the fuse, the paper flutters down before his eyes. Startled, he reads it. His eyes open wide – now he realizes the danger!

Blue Beard orders the crew to take away half the barrels. When they are done he stoops, lights the fuse and runs with his crew down the tunnel.

Go to page 22

This tunnel is short. After just a few paces it opens out into a cave. It's amazing! You see chests overflowing with gold, stacked all around the walls. Sitting alone at the centre of all the gold is the fiercest pirate you have ever seen. His eyes are black, his teeth are black and so is his beard. But somehow he looks lonely and sad.

You step forward. Black Beard sees you!

Go to page 43 

Before you can stop yourself you say, “That’s wrong!” Luckily the pirates are arguing so loudly they don’t hear you, though one looks round.

But it is you who are wrong! Red Beard got his calculation right.

$$\begin{array}{r|l} & \ \ 13 \\ \hline 15 & 200 \\ & -15 \\ \hline & \ \ \ 50 \\ & -45 \\ \hline & \ \ \ \ 5 \text{ remainder} \end{array}$$

Go to page 17

You shuffle along the ledge. As the ledge gets narrower and narrower, your heart beats faster and faster. Suddenly there is nothing under your foot. The ledge has ended!

You almost lose your balance and fall, but you just manage to cling to the rocks.

You chose the wrong direction. The answer to the ‘right’ sum is 7890. Check the answer to the ‘left’ sum and see if it is greater.

Go to page 13

Ahead the passage narrows again, but you can see a light flickering at the end. You hear the sound of voices and the clink of coins. It’s the pirate band. They are sharing out their loot!

You press against the tunnel wall and creep towards the light. Suddenly you feel a gap. There is a side passage you had not spotted! You slip inside and look around.

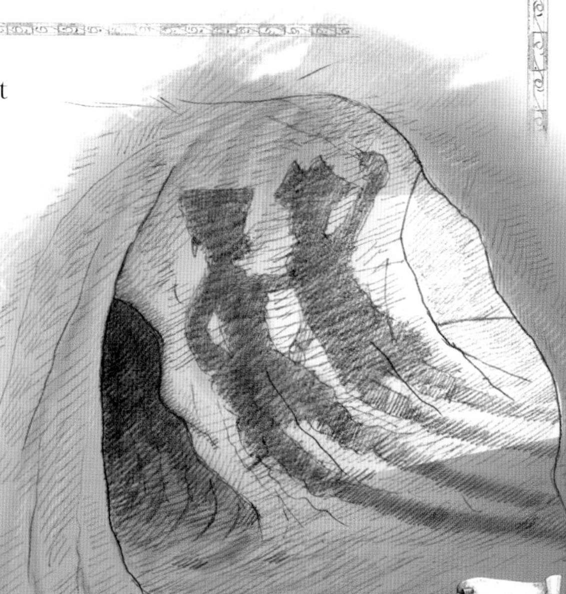

Go to page 15

You are wrong! There are 14 barrels with 3.5 kg in each barrel. You must calculate 3.5×14.

$3.5 \times 10 = 35$ and $3.5 \times 4 = 14$, so $3.5 \times 14 = 35 + 14 = 49$. 49 kg is nearly twice the safe amount. The whole tunnel will collapse!

Go to page 10 

You turn left and follow the passage. It gets narrower. The floor is covered with loose rocks. Small stones are falling from above. Suddenly you hear a rumble and a crash. It's a rock slide! Your lamp goes out in the dust. Then you hear a squawking sound. It leads you to safety around the fallen boulders.

You chose the wrong direction! The decimal 0.4 is equal to 40%, but the fraction $\frac{1}{4}$ is 25%, or 0.25.

Go to page 4

You add the number 52 to the list in your notebook. But somehow it doesn't seem to fit. Suddenly, a slimy green tentacle bursts through the lid of the barrel and slithers towards your leg!

Just in time you kick the barrel over the side. Bubbles rise as it sinks into the depths.

You cross out the 52. It was the wrong number.

Go to page 12

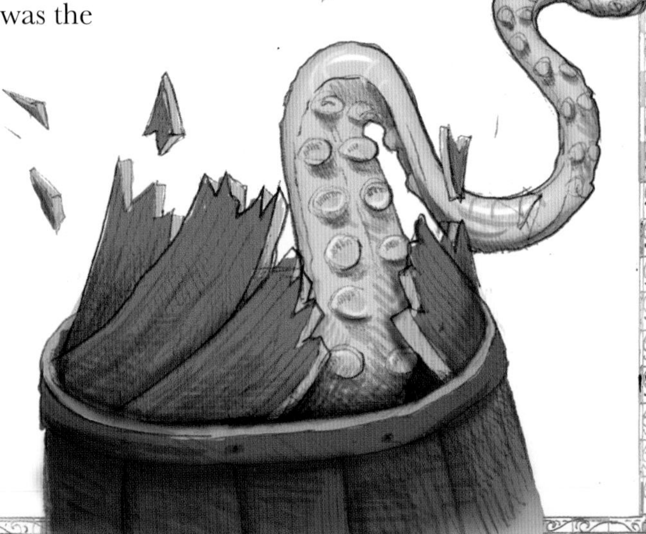

It's the wrong gap! The way ahead is completely blocked! The pirates are starting to climb the rubble heap!

A good estimate for 39×61 is $40 \times 60 = 2400$. Use your calculator to check that 39×61 is closer to 2400 than to 2500.

Go to page 14 

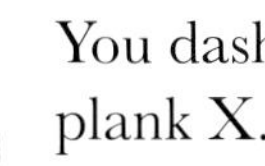

You dash across the bridge, taking care not to step on plank X. You were right! You are safely on the other side.

Blue Beard follows you across the bridge. He avoids plank Y but steps on X. (His maths is not as good as yours!) The plank snaps and the bridge collapses. Blue Beard climbs back up the hanging bridge to the tunnel mouth. You smile and wave back as he shakes his fist angrily on the other side of the gorge.

Go to page 8 

You use your finger to write the numbers 350 and 1000 in the spaces. A huge hairy leg steps out onto the web. For a moment you think you must be wrong. But the leg pulls a thread, and a gap opens in the web. You rush through. They were the right numbers!

Go to page 9 

It's the correct direction! As you shuffle along the ledge it gradually gets wider. Soon you are able to walk more easily. Your heart beat starts to return to normal.

Then you see a gap in the rock wall. It's a doorway! The entrance is blocked by a padlocked rusty iron gate.

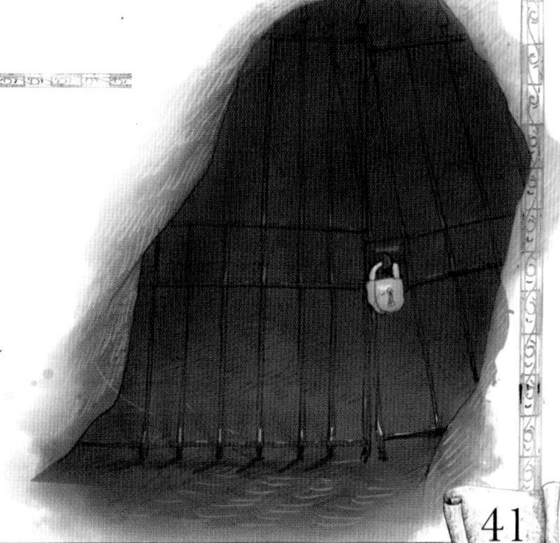

Go to page 16 

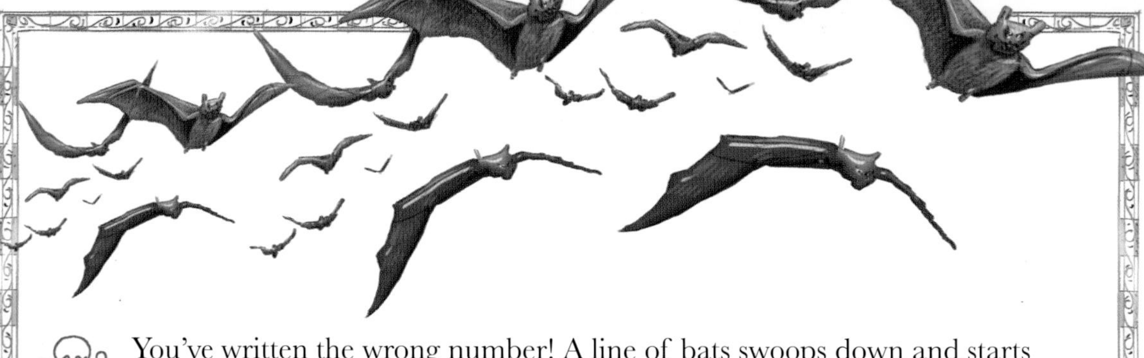

You've written the wrong number! A line of bats swoops down and starts circling around you. They are getting closer and closer! Then, a flurry of bright feathers flies at the bats. It frightens them away! What was that?

The number 70 is 20 more than 50. So, if you subtract 70 from 150 you are left with 80. What is 80 – 68?

Go to page 30

You race down the tunnel. Ahead you can see that it opens out into a large cave full of mining tools. There are pickaxes and shovels, stacks of logs to prop up the roof, and rusty old trucks on rails for carrying rocks. You made the right choice.

Go to page 29 

You step on stone 8 × 4. It starts to wobble. You are going to fall into the red-hot lava! Just as you lose your balance, a claw grabs your collar and gives a tug. You manage to straighten and step back onto stone 6 × 6. Who was that helping you?

6 × 6 = 36. The other stones you need are part of the 12 and 4 times tables.

Go to page 23 

As you lift down the torch, its flame flickers and dies. The other torches start to fade, too. You are going to be stranded in the dark!

Quickly you put the torch back. The remaining torches brighten again. 6 × 7 = 42. What is 7 × 7?

Go to page 26 

You climb aboard a truck on the right track and push off. The truck rolls down a sloping track into a narrow tunnel. You are heading in the right direction. But everything seems abandoned – perhaps all the diamonds were found long ago. Then you hear loud voices ahead. There are pirates down there!

Go to page 20 

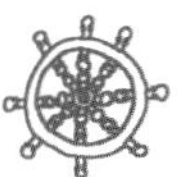

"Welcome, shipmate!" cries Black Beard. "Come here and share my gold!"

You see the shining gold buckle on the belt that crosses his chest. It's the fourth pirate sign! But Pollygone ruffles her feathers and screeches, "Stay back! Stay back!" You see that Black Beard is surrounded by four circles of rope. Four knots hold the rope ends together. A message pinned to the barrel explains everything...

The Pirates' Curse

You can keep your stolen things,
While you are in the pirate rings.
But cross the ropes, and you'll turn to dust,
And all your gold will turn to rust.
You can never step outside
While the pirates' knots are tied.

Black Beard wants to trick you into stepping inside the ropes, so he can escape!

Go to page 27 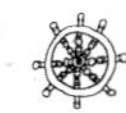

Calculation words

addition

When you add you find the total of two or more numbers. The symbol for addition is the plus sign +. Most people learn to add by counting on. If you start with the number seven and count on by three, you get to ten – you have added three to seven. As you learn your 'number bonds' you no longer need to count on – you will just know that seven plus three is ten.

You can add larger numbers by setting them out like this:

Th	H	T	U	
4	4	1	5	
3	5	3	6	+
7	9	5	1	
		1		

decimal

Decimal means 'made from groups of ten'. The decimal number 12.5 has 1 ten, 2 units and 5 tenths. The digit after the decimal point is not a whole number but a fraction. The decimal fraction 0.6 is the same as 'six tenths' or $\frac{6}{10}$.

division

When you divide you find out how many times one number can be shared out, or divided up, by another number. The symbol for division is the division sign ÷. When you know your times tables then you can divide as well as multiply. If you know that 4 × 5 = 20, then you also know that 20 ÷ 4 = 5.

If one number cannot be divided exactly by another number then there is a remainder: 9 ÷ 4 = 2 remainder 1.

You can divide larger numbers (for example 200 ÷ 15) by setting them out as a long division:

```
     13
15 | 200
    -15
     50
    - 45
      5 remainder
```

doubles
When you double a number you multiply it by 2. This is the same as adding the number to itself. For example:

double eight = $2 \times 8 = 16$
double eight = $8 + 8 = 16$

estimate/estimation
When you have a long calculation to make, such as 103×29, it is good to estimate the answer before you start. Then you will know if you have made a serious mistake when you do the calculation carefully. An estimate is a quick calculation which gives you an answer close to the accurate answer.

To make an estimate, round the numbers to make them easier to work with. A good estimate for 103×29 is $100 \times 30 = 3000$. The accurate answer is 2987.

fraction
A fraction is a number that is less than one. Half is a fraction. Half a pizza is less than a whole pizza.

The fraction $\frac{3}{10}$ means that the whole is divided into ten equal parts and you have three of these parts. A fraction written in this way ($\frac{3}{10}$) is called a vulgar fraction.

You can also write fractions as decimal fractions (0.3 in this case).

$$\frac{3}{10} = 0.3$$

Three-tenths of the shape are grey.

To convert a vulgar fraction to a decimal fraction you divide the numerator (the number above the line) by the denominator (the number below the line). Use a calculator or long division.

$$\frac{1}{4} = 1 \div 4 = 0.25$$

multiplication

When you multiply six by four you increase the six by four times: four lots of six are twenty-four. The symbol for multiplication is ×. If you know all your times tables you know how to multiply any two numbers up to 10 × 10. You can multiply larger numbers by setting them out as a long multiplication like this:

Th	H	T	U	
	2	1	4	
			6	×
1	2	8	4	
1		2		

number line

A number line shows numbers spaced out in order. It is useful for comparing one number to another. From this line you can see that 50 is half way between 0 and 100, so 50 is half the size of 100. You can use a number line to help with calculations by counting on or back along it.

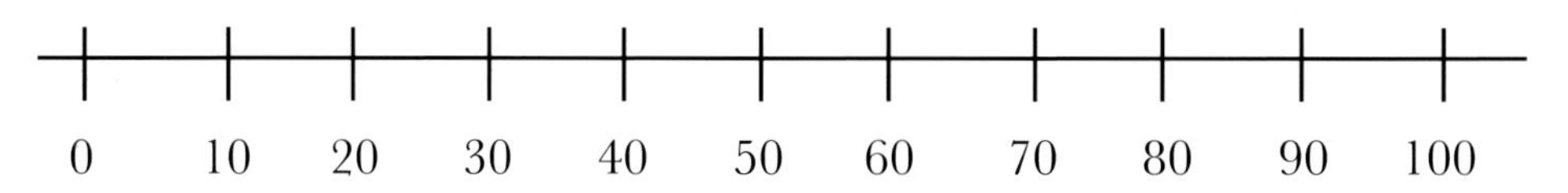

percentage

A percentage is another way for giving fractions of a whole. One per cent of something is one hundredth part. The symbol for percentage is %. One hundred per cent (100%) is the whole. Fifty per cent (50%) is fifty hundredths, which is the same as half. Ten per cent (10%) is ten hundredths, which is one tenth. When you divide something into parts, the percentages of the different parts must all add up to 100 % – the whole.

To convert a decimal fraction or a vulgar fraction to a percentage you multiply by 100.

$$0.5 = \frac{1}{2} \times 100\% = 50\%$$

$$0.4 = \frac{2}{5} \times 100\% = 40\%$$

subtraction

When you subtract you take one number away from another. The answer is the difference between the numbers. The symbol for subtraction is the minus sign –. You can subtract by counting back. If you start with the number seven and count back three, you get to four – you have subtracted three from seven. As you learn your 'number bonds' you no longer need to count back – you will just know that seven minus three is four.

You can subtract larger numbers by setting them out like this:

Th	H	T	U	
4	3	[4] ~~5~~	[1] 1	
4	2	2	7	–
	1	2	4	

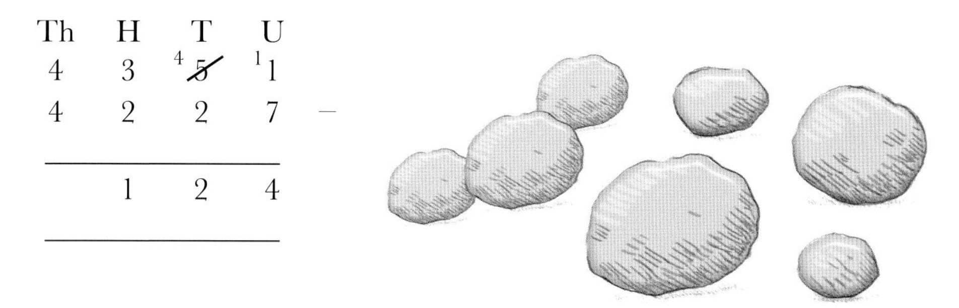

times tables

To become a good mathematician you must learn your times tables. Then you will be able to solve multiplication problems quickly and easily. This multiplication square contains all the times tables up to 10. To find the answer to 6 × 8 you find the 6 in the top row and the 8 in the left column. The answer is in the square where the column below the 6 and the row from the 8 meet.

×	1	2	3	4	5	6	7	8	9	10
1	1	2	3	4	5	6	7	8	9	10
2	2	4	6	8	10	12	14	16	18	20
3	3	6	9	12	15	18	21	24	27	30
4	4	8	12	16	20	24	28	32	36	40
5	5	10	15	20	25	30	35	40	45	50
6	6	12	18	24	30	36	42	48	54	60
7	7	14	21	28	35	42	49	56	63	70
8	8	16	24	32	40	**48**	56	64	72	80
9	9	18	27	36	45	54	63	72	81	90
10	10	20	30	40	50	60	70	80	90	100

Notes for parents and teachers

The Maths Quest series of books is designed to motivate children to develop and apply their maths skills through engaging adventure stories. The stories work as games in which the children must solve a series of mathematical problems to make progress towards the exciting conclusion.

The books do not follow a conventional pattern. The reader is directed to jump forwards and back through the book according to the answers they give to the problems. If their answers are correct, they make progress to the next part of the story; if they are incorrect the mathematics is explained, before the reader is directed back to try the problem again. Additional support may be found in the glossary at the back of the book.

To support your child's mathematical development you can:

- Read the book with your child.

- Solve the initial problems and discover how the book works.

- Continue reading with your child until he or she is using the book confidently, following the **Go to** instructions to find the next puzzle or explanation.

- Encourage your child to read on alone. Ask "What's happening now?" Prompt your child to tell you how the story develops and what problems they have solved.

- Discuss numbers in everyday contexts: shopping, filling up the car at the garage; looking at the car mileage and road signs when on journeys; using timetables; following recipes and so on.

- Have fun making up number sequences and patterns. Count in 2s, 3s, 4s and 5s and larger steps. Ask times-table questions to pass the time on journeys. Count backwards in different steps. List doubles, halves, square numbers and primes. Play "I'm thinking of a number, can you guess it?" games in which you ask questions such as "Is it even or odd?", "Is it bigger than 100?", "How many digits does it have?" and so on.

- Play number-based computer games with your child. These will hold children's interest with colourful graphics and lively animations as they practise basic number skills.

- Most of all, make maths fun!